ONCE MORE TO THE RIVER

FAMILY SNAPSHOTS OF GROWING UP, GETTING OUT AND GOING BACK

ERASMO GUERRA

"Childhood's End" was originally published in *Texas Monthly*. "Freedom Ride" and "Once More to the River" first appeared in *The Texas Observer*. "Once More to the River" was also included in *Hecho en Tejas*, edited by Dagoberto Gilb. "Tex-Mex Express" ran in *ColorLines*. "Recuerdo: My Sister Remembered" first appeared in the collection *Fifteen Candles: Fifteen Tales of Taffeta, Hairspray, Drunk Uncles, and other Quinceañera Stories*, edited by Adriana Lopez.

Cover design by New Design Lab: newdesignlab.com
Cover photograph from the author's collection

To contact the author:
Times Square Station
P.O. Box 224
New York, NY 10108

ISBN: 1480223735
ISBN-13: 978-1480223738

For my mother
Maria Guadalupe Guerra

CONTENTS

INTRODUCTION

Many nights, my mom stood on the front porch and hollered at my sister, brother and me to get home after we spent the day wandering the neighborhood. She called us *desvalagados*. Not exactly lost, but loose.

She didn't like us spending too much time in "borrowed houses."

"There's nothing like your own home," Mom said. *"No hay más como tu propia casa."*

And there never will be. Although I've lived in New York City for nearly two decades, when I sit down at my writing desk I still hear my mom's echoes and return to that stretch of the Texas-Mexico border along the Rio Grande where I was born and raised.

These stories first appeared in magazines, online journals and literary anthologies, but this book gathers them together in a proper collection of their own.

Childhood's End

My childhood ended the summer I was seventeen and working the counter at the Pecos Bill Tall Tale Inn and Cafe at Walt Disney World's Frontierland. I wore black garters on the sleeves of the candy-striped, button-down shirt that served as a uniform, but otherwise this was just a glorified fast-food gig no different from working at Whataburger. Over the clatter of Big Thunder Mountain Railroad—and the screams of all the thrill-seeking riders—I filled drink orders and got yelled at by moms from Buffalo who'd asked for no beans in their taco salad.

I'd never seen a taco salad in my life. I was from Mission, Texas, birthplace of legendary Dallas Cowboys coach Tom Landry, where the only cafe I knew was called Pepe's. I'd spent previous summers working at a photography studio, washing the large windows at the downtown chamber of commerce, and cleaning out mobile home trailers for $50 each. What I really dreamed of doing? I could never really say. Growing up the middle child in what seemed like the middle of nowhere, all I knew was that I shouldn't want too much.

That summer of 1987, I went to Florida to live with second cousins, and got hired at Disney. I think they stuck me in the Pecos Bill simply because I was from Texas. The Disney laundry service provided crisp Western shirts at the start of each shift, but I wasn't much into playing "cowboys." My mom had tried dressing me up in country-western "kicker" drag from Mission Dry Goods, but I always felt as ridiculous as a member of the Village People.

Among my high school classmates, the trend was Roper boots, but I was a loner geek who continued wearing his penny loafers and second-hand clothes bought by the pound from the local *ropa usada*. My stylish older sister Michelle hardly approved. A cheerleader, school paper staffer, and homecoming queen also-ran, my sister had big hair, a huge smile, and impossible dreams of getting out.

Our overprotective parents made it hard for her to go anywhere other than chaperoned school trips. None of us were allowed to stay out later than ten o'clock. She hollered for most of her life that she couldn't wait to finish high school and leave. But until then, she made efforts to fit in, joining the Future Farmers of America and raising a sheep that sold to a local slaughterhouse at the Mercedes Livestock Show. She slipped in and out of her school-club jackets and sequined gowns with all the ease of the professional model and actress she hoped to become one day.

I had no real ambitions of my own—at least I never admitted them like she did—and blindly followed when she signed up for drama class, thinking it'd be an easy A. I must have also thought I'd get her approval. I landed every male lead and placed at local speech tournaments, outshining my sister, but only on stage. On campus, I was still a bit of a loser, with just a friend or two, while she maintained an almost oppressive popularity.

I can't say going to Florida was my conscious attempt to set myself free, but maybe my sister's ceaseless rebel call to "get out" had stirred me to run off ahead as she continued the battle at home.

Michelle had graduated that summer and fought to go upstate for college, but because she was a girl, my parents felt she'd be safer in the Valley, where she could attend the local commuter college that everyone derided as Taco Tech. I felt sorry for her, guilty that I had more freedom because I was a boy.

But mostly I missed her, and my little brother, Marco. This was the first time I'd been away from both of them, the first time I'd ever left Texas. I was reminded of it each time I turned on the radio. The rock ballad "Alone," by Heart, was a huge hit that summer and everywhere I went the Wilson sisters wailed, pounded the keyboards, and pulled the strings of their electric guitars as if they were my own veins. I grew increasingly homesick, recalling the grumbling crop-dusters that banked low over our *colonia* as they made repeated sweeps of the nearby fields, hot afternoons spent making backyard "swimming pools" out of heavy garbage bags, and trying to finish rainbow-colored *raspas* before they melted into a brown puddle.

The weekend of the Fourth of July, my Florida cousins went off to a Sunday barbecue. I stayed at the house, listening to firecrackers and illicit gunshots, eventually crying myself to sleep to memories of childhood sparklers that never burned out. A neighborhood dog howled throughout the night.

The following morning, I was awakened by a knock at my bedroom door. Mom was on the phone long distance. She said Michelle was missing.

My sister, who'd been to a cookout with her boyfriend, had come home the previous night to an empty house. Mom was cashiering a late shift at the H.E.B. grocery store. Dad and Marco were at the family ranch. By the time everyone returned home, my sister's Camaro was still in the driveway, but she was gone.

When I arrived home the next day, Michelle still hadn't turned up and I spent the afternoon driving Dad's pickup truck around town, posting flyers that read "HAVE YOU SEEN HER?"

At dusk, my sister was found, her murdered body abandoned in a mesquite-studded pasture behind our house. I shouted her name into the darkness, trying to pry myself loose of every hand holding onto me as I struggled to reach the backyard fence and, just beyond, the flashlight beams cutting through the dry grass.

★

At my age, I'd attended a few funerals, including those of my dad's parents, but this was the first time I was forced to make the arrangements. My parents just couldn't. So on a rainy morning, lulled by the squeaky wipers smearing the windshield, I rode with a sales agent from Valley Memorial Gardens to the mortuary. I picked out a casket with interior upholstery a lighter shade of pink than my sister's bedroom walls. I remember thinking how much I wanted Michelle to like what I'd picked out for her.

★

After the burial, our house went silent, feeling as locked up as a roadside fireworks stand now closed for the season. We blamed ourselves for not being home the night of my sister's initial disappearance, but as the one who'd been the farthest away, the guilt left me feeling even more alone amid the family. Restless, I rode back to Florida with my cousins, who'd made the cross-country drive to offer their condolences. I never reported back to the Pecos Bill. Instead, through a neighbor, I got hired at a local nursery, where I pruned and repotted and shipped out orders of ivy, hibiscus and lilies of the valley.

I worked long hours in sweaty, suffocating greenhouses, ate brown-bag lunches with immigrant co-workers, and then waited out the terrible thunderstorms that rolled through every late afternoon before heading home. Having come from sturdy *norteño* stock, laborers who could barely scratch an X for their name, I told myself this was where I belonged, with my hands in the dirt—not in front of the painted backdrops of a fantasyland amusement park.

My sister's murderer was never found. When I returned to school for my senior year, I kept a tearless, resentful front. I pushed everyone away, focusing on schoolwork and the speech and drama tournaments, ultimately winning the state championship medal. It was the first time in 25 years that anyone from our school had won anything at state, but I didn't take much joy in it, and my parents barely noticed. I received an appointment to the United States Military Academy at West Point and was set to report for summer Beast Barracks in June.

At my high school graduation ceremony, held out on the football field that once echoed with my sister's cheers, I could no longer contain my sorrow, and so after tossing up my tasseled hat, I huddled with my family and cried under the harsh stadium lights. Fellow students and their families kept their distance—and I have, too. I haven't spent another summer in South Texas since.

FREEDOM RIDE

My bus is called. Outside the station, the noon air smells of exhaust and escape—the oily heaviness of leaving or being left—and I get in line behind the other passengers traveling from the Valley to San Antonio.

A solid, middle-aged woman with a bad dye-job and perm grabs my bags and tosses them into the cargo hold beneath the bus. The driver takes my flimsy accordion of tickets, rips out the boarding pass, and lets me on.

Moments later, as people are still getting seated, I hear my mother call out to the driver. She wants to make sure I haven't gotten on the wrong bus.

"No, ma'am," he assures her. "This bus is going to San Antonio."

"It's that I heard it was headed to Reynosa," she says.

The last thing my mother wants is for me to wind up in Mexico, which, in her news-saturated imagination, is about as good as sending me across the river to be made into breakfast tacos.

Never mind that I'm in my 30s and have been living in the tough city of New York for more than a decade. This ride to San Antonio stirs up all her wild fears of bus-jackings and, more than likely, the dirty old men who hang out in station bathrooms.

I stand up, searching for my mother through the windows, hoping she won't decide to come into the bus for a weepy farewell. Other than her voice still ringing in my ears, there is no sign of her. I spot my father standing inside the station. A moment later, my mother joins him. They remain by the windows looking out.

The driver, whose nametag reads "Jesus," stands at the front end of the aisle and counts the number of available seats. His forehead sweaty, he runs his fingers through his gray hair as if trying to untangle a problem.

The baggage handler boards the bus. Her face is splattered with freckles and moles, and her jaw drops as she makes an announcement, first in Spanish and then English: "There is one person here who has a ticket for tomorrow. Please raise your hand." No one moves.

"There are also five of you who were supposed to leave on the 9:15 and didn't. Please show your hands." Nothing.

"Because of you, there are people who bought tickets for this bus and aren't able to get on because there are no more seats. *Por favor*, board those buses you have tickets for; otherwise we run into these kinds of problems."

She comes down the aisle and stops next to a *vaquero* wearing diamond horseshoe rings on both hands. His straw hat and bag take up the seat next to him. She tells him to please remove his bag. When it looks like he's not listening, she grips his things, stuffs them into the overhead bin, and then turns to everyone and huffs that we should remove our belongings from the empty seats so that other people may sit.

As she comes further down the aisle, she stops at a quiet old lady with a long, gray braid down her back. She looks like someone who, up until now, has only traveled by *huarache* or burro. The baggage handler calls to the driver, "This woman's got tortillas all over her seat."

She must have bought them that morning at a *tortillería* and was trying to air them out so that they wouldn't stick together. The driver tells the old lady to please pack up her tortillas so that another passenger can sit.

A young mother and her little girl are forced to take the final two front seats across the aisle from each other. The passengers on either side of them refuse to move. The disabled vet is willing, despite the fact that he's wearing a combat boot on one foot and a cast on the other. But the woman in the other seat won't sit with him. So mother and child sit apart.

Across from me, a middle-aged woman reaches under her cantaloupe-colored T-shirt and unsnaps her bra and then flips through the pages of a *Reader's Digest* with a cover story that reads: "The Hidden Danger of Healthy Foods."

Jesus shuts the bus door and goes back into the station. A guy in a "Young Country 103.5 FM" giveaway T-shirt comes down the aisle to get off for a smoke. But now he can't open the door.

La Comadre Cantaloupe says, *"Ya te quedaste adentro."*

"'Orita quiebro una ventana," he says, stomping back to his seat.

Someone in back starts signaling the driver. Maybe it's the Tortilla Lady, who asks the man next to her, "What time are we going to arrive in San Antonio?"

"Four o'clock," he says.

"So when am I going to arrive in Dallas?"

"I say around nine tonight."

Tortilla Lady sighs and calls out the names of a few saints to give her patience. She taps at the window so that we can get a move on and then turns back to the man. *"Hacen mucha caña,"* she says.

La Comadre shows her *Reader's Digest* to the woman sitting next to her.

"I read it, too, but in Spanish," the other woman says.

"Me in English and Spanish," La Comadre says. "Though at times I don't understand many words in Spanish."

The other woman says she knows nothing in English.

"Ay, they have such good stories," La Comadre says. "And recipes."

"And jokes," the other adds.

"I've had this one for a while because I just haven't made the time." She puts the magazine face down on her lap. "Did you watch television last night?" She mentions the name of a reality show. "It's getting good."

The other woman says she doesn't watch much TV. "It's that I work nights," she says. She works at a bakery, packing *pan dulce* that gets shipped to the local schools and as far away as Laredo. She also works at the El Pato on Old Highway 83 in McAllen.

La Comadre nods and says she likes the TV programs on Channel 12. She names a few shows that sound like *telenovelas*. "But at times they irritate me because the stories are so mixed up."

When Jesus gets back on the bus, settling behind the wheel, the two women quiet down. He slaps the horn, and we pull out of the station. My mother has come out to the boarding area, waving and blowing kisses to everyone on the bus, directing her affection at each tinted window because she can't see where I'm sitting.

La Comadre and the other woman agree, *"El que se quedó, se quedó."*

Once on the highway, they turn to the window and remark how pretty everything looks.

"¡Oyes, sí!" La Comadre says.

We're in Pharr, banking an overpass that heads north, and all around us in a soft haze the Valley seems to fall away as if we are flying on an airplane. Both women say, *"Las matas, qué bonitas,"* referring to the palms and bougainvillea.

★

The young mother in front tells the driver about her ordeal, how they told her to go to the Harlingen station when she was in Weslaco. From Harlingen she rode to McAllen, where they told her, sorry, the bus is full.

She shakes her head and smoothes out the wrinkles of a pink and green serape folded over her lap. She smiles at her little girl in the next seat, bare brown legs swinging, Power Puff Girl *chanclas* on her feet.

She asks her mother, "Can y'gimme my orange juice?"

It's really orange soda.

The girl takes a sip and hands it back. She wipes her mouth with the entire length of her brown arm, from her downy shoulder to her skinny wrist, and says she's full.

The mother puts the soda away and then fixes her ponytail. She wears gold hoop earrings, a black sleeveless blouse, and sweat pants that match her New Balance sneakers. She looks all of 20 and alone.

La Comadre's seatmate gets off in Edinburg. A big guy, chewing gum, wearing tight black Wranglers, takes the other woman's place. On his lap he has a slim hardback titled *Attitude 101.*

Ready to get back on the road, Jesus hollers to Mister Young Country, who had stepped off the bus for a quick smoke.

"Turn off the *cigarro* and let's go," he says. *"Vámonos."*

"That's it?" Young Country says, stalling. "No more passengers?"

Jesus responds with impatient silence.

"Well, I was just waiting for the others."

Jesus, still not saying anything, stares out the door until the guy comes inside. As he walks down the aisle, the stench of cigarettes trails him.

Fanning away the smoke, the young mother tells the vet about her life. "I was studying for medical records," she says. "I got certified and worked at a hospital, but I didn't like it. Didn't like the paperwork."

She turns to her little girl and asks if she's hungry. "You want some tacos?" She nods at the same time to convince the girl that, yes, she wants one. "Your grandma made you tacos."

The girl says okay. The mother searches her bag and pulls out a greasy, foil-wrapped mess. The girl takes a single bite and hands it back.

"Don't want no more?"

The girl shakes her head.

The mother re-wraps the taco and then turns to the vet. "D'you hear that if you eat meat you get cancer?" She shakes her head. "Can't eat this. Can't eat that."

The girl asks for a bag of Funyuns. The mother hands it to her. The girl puts the bag between her dusty knees and pulls out one Funyun ring after another.

As we approach the border checkpoint in Falfurrias, the young mother makes the sign of the cross and kisses her thumb. She looks over and smiles at her little girl. Jesus slows down. The bus shudders and groans as we join the line of vehicles.

La Comadre looks out the window and complains, "This looks like Reynosa. What's going on here?" She jokes with the guy next to her, "If they take you off, I don't know you."

I hear a woman behind me reassure another rider that if there are any questions, a driver's license should be fine. "It's enough at the bridge," she says.

The signs along the road instruct us to dim our headlights; these are federal agents, we are told. Further up they announce that dogs are on duty. The biggest sign posts the year-to-date seizures:

Drugs
49,833 lbs
Undocumented Aliens
7,350

All my life, anytime I traveled outside of the Valley, I endured this final moment. The agent stared you down behind his black-tinted aviator sunglasses; tapped your car door to test for the sound of drugs being smuggled in the panels; and asked where you're coming from and where you're going and whether you're an American citizen.

My mother always warned us to answer with a smile. I always offered a resentful yes. As the years go by, I've seen my beloved South Texas homeland become a militarized zone of border agents who not only stop you at the river and as far as 50 miles north, but also cruise our neighborhoods in their window-tinted vehicles.

So I don't know why I think they'll just pass us through this afternoon.

They don't.

Jesus steers the bus off to the right, under a tree where another Greyhound has been parked and emptied. For a moment I panic that those passengers have all been lined up and shot. I get this terrible feeling in my gut. A murmur of fear ripples down the rows of seats.

The little girl asks, "Mommy, what're we doing?"

"Stopping because they have to check the bus."

Without making an announcement, Jesus gets off. The bus rocks as the luggage compartments are yanked open for the dogs to sniff out any contraband. Two agents in their military greens appear at the head of the bus aisle. One stands with a panting German shepherd on a leash. The other agent comes down the rows, pointing at individual passengers and asking, "U.S. citizen?"

When he turns to the little girl, the mother speaks up. "She's my daughter," she says. Which doesn't really answer the question.

The woman next to the girl says, "American."

La Comadre says, "Yes, sir, U.S. of A." Just as my mother would.

All I say is yes.

The young mother, struggling with a smile that is not a smile, eyes the dog and then looks up at the agent holding the leash.

She pleads, "It's not gonna bite me, right?"

The agent says no.

From the bottom of the stairs, Jesus calls, "All clear?"

The agents take a final look at us and, heading back out, they tell Jesus he can go.

★

Back on the road, the young mother chews her gum so hard I expect the crack of a molar to sound off like a gunshot. She turns to the little girl and says, "That was fun, right?"

"What?" the little girl says—even at her young age she's not convinced. She doesn't know what her mother means by "that was fun."

"The dog," she says, snapping her gum and looking out to the road ahead.

★

We continue north on Highway 281. Harsh sunlight glints off the chrome of speeding SUV's and southbound semi-trucks making deliveries to Wal-Mart and H.E.B. "Go Home A Hero," reads the side of one truck.

The bus rushes alongside pastures of high, dry grass, and fenced wilderness of huizache and mesquite and sagebrush. We dip and buck as we push forward. Nearing San Antonio, the Hemisfair Tower in the distance, Jesus clicks on the intercom and wakes us with a grand announcement.

"Damas y caballeros—," he begins.

We have arrived.

TEX-MEX EXPRESS

At the San Antonio bus station, the Americanos bus idled in lane two. I got on line behind a young veteran on crutches, a desert-camouflage rucksack on his back that read "National Guardsmen Since 1836." Overhead announcements continued to blare for the McAllen-Brownsville-Matamoros route now boarding.

A second-generation Texas-Mexican, I grew up on the U.S.-Mexico border and have been living in New York City for the past 16 years. All last year I kept up with the papers and watched the nightly reports about the increasing border violence and the spread of swine flu. I endured the fear mongers who insisted on more agents, even troops, and those who made taco jokes at our expense. Even my mother, who still lived in the Rio Grande Valley, made me wince when she admitted in her Sunday night phone calls that things back home had "gotten *bien* ugly."

I remembered a different place, where *panaderías* sold gingerbread pig cookies and going across the border was just a routine, care-free activity to buy birthday piñatas and string puppets for us kids, discount cartons of Salems for my father and sacks of candied pumpkin for my mother.

So while I was in San Antonio recently, I decided to head back to see just how bad and broken the border was.

Climbing aboard the bus, I nearly tore my pressed, button-down shirt on a jerry-rigged clothes hanger sticking out of the inside panel of the front door. It's something I wouldn't have noticed growing up because do-it-yourself fixes were such a regular part of our make-do life along the border. We baked enchiladas with blocks of government cheese, insulated house windows with aluminum foil and drove around with gallon jugs of water in our used cars to pour into overheated radiators.

On the bus, I took a seat in the second row, and a young couple with a toddler took the seat behind me—only the man explained to the driver, "M'just dropping her off, sir."

The couple kissed, and the man reassured the woman, "Call y'later." On his way back out, he told the driver, "*Dios lo bendiga.*"

The young woman pulled her daughter to the window and went through a mom and daughter ventriloquist act, saying, "Bye, Papi. I love you."

Our driver, wearing a white button-down shirt, black clip-on tie hanging to one side, chatted in Spanish with one of the other drivers. They commiserated about their nagging coughs, speaking of them as if they were women they couldn't shake. "*N'hombre, hasta limón con miel l'hecho—y no me deja,*" one said.

Just as our driver was about to shut the door and take us on our way, the other driver called out, "*Tienes uno más.*" A Mexican-Mexican, as we used to say, meaning he was from across the river. Wearing a pair of Wranglers, a straw cowboy hat in his hands, the man stood quietly at the bottom of the staircase.

"*Vámonos,*" the driver hollered before the man even dared come aboard.

He took a seat in the front row, but not before politely asking the driver if it was okay to sit there. "*Cómo que no,*" the driver said and got behind the wheel.

Pulling out of the station and into the downtown streets, the young mother was already phoning the man she'd left behind, alternately scolding her daughter—"*Gorda, siéntate, porque vamos ir* b'bye!"—and pulling her over to speak on the cell phone with her daddy.

I looked over at the man who'd come in last. I've always been startled by men like these—men like my father, who grew up picking cotton and was weathered from too much work in the sun, his skin now like that of a battered leather wallet, but who still managed to clean up good.

This man wore a gray polo that matched his trim mustache and his salt-and-pepper hair. His straw hat looked so pristine that he might've just bought it for that trip south. He looked, as we say, *bien arregla'o, bien planchadito.* It would've made any mama proud. It's why I'd dressed up, too.

As the miles ticked off and the landscape went from suburban monotony to dense thickets of mesquite and nopal, I didn't think we'd make so much as a stop during the four-hour ride down to the Valley. But in Falfurrias, just before the border checkpoint and 50 miles from the border wall that was still being built, the bus pulled into one of those sprawling service stations, and the driver announced, "Fifteen minutes. *Quince minutos.*"

★

After the break, all of us back in our seats and ready to get back on the road, the driver couldn't get the door closed. He used one hand to pull the wire hanger and the other to push a button on the dashboard.

"*Ay, puertita,*" he said, as he tried again and the hydraulic mechanism failed with a defeated sigh.

He turned to the Mexican in the gray shirt and explained that he'd been assured he wouldn't have trouble with the door. He was told he'd make it all the way to Matamoros. "*Allí estan los mecánicos,*" he said.

While the driver pulled on the door, the Mexican pushed the dashboard button, and the rest of us sat in silence—except for la Gorda, who began to act up and got a new name to match her bad behavior. "*Pórtate bien, Chiflada,*" her mother snapped.

We needed more than the blessing we'd been given at the start of the trip, so the driver got off in search of help and returned with a crowbar. Back inside the bus, he tried to pry the door shut, while outside a much older man and two kids, whom I took to be his grandchildren, watched. They were dressed in camouflage, the old man standing tall in a hunter's cap, as if they were on their way to shoot *paloma, venado or javelina.*

This was what I'd come for: to see these faces and hear these voices all around me. It proved that we were still the people I knew us to be, not the terrible outlaws they reported on TV, which I had nearly believed. Having been away from home for so many years and so many miles, I was being reminded as I drew closer to the border that even when certain things in our life circumstances seemed broken, our spirit wasn't.

Once the bus door was forced shut, the crowbar was passed through the driver's window to the grandfather and the kids and the young father who came around later—all three generations of one South Texas family.

Starting the bus engine, the driver called to the Mexican behind him. "*Gracías por tu ayuda.*"

"*No, pos, de nada,*" the Mexican said with the typical humility that has always bewildered my American need to take credit.

But it was more than nothing. He'd brought us that much closer to getting home. And for the rest of the ride, I was hopeful that we'd figure a way to hold it together and keep going.

ONCE MORE TO THE RIVER

Each summer, as a young girl, Maria Guadalupe crossed the Rio Grande into Mexico to spend the long months at the ranch that belonged to her family. They rode to the riverbank by taxi, steered by her *tío* Garcia. "He was fat," she says, which is all she remembers about him and the drive to the Los Ebanos Ferry, which she calls *el chalán*.

Her father never went. None of her brothers remember going either, though she insists that they did. It may have just been the women: Maria and her sister Belsa, their mother Victorina, and their aunt Petra and cousin Elvita. The taxi would leave them at the river, and they would board the hand-pulled ferry on foot.

The ferry is named after the surrounding community of Los Ebanos, which is named after the Texas ebony, a thorny tree with horned-moon husks; white-wing doves nest in its branches; the black-brown seeds are eaten by wild, tusked pigs. Los Ebanos is one of those communities that upstate folks cannot resist calling "sleepy" and "quiet."

The truth is that everyone is miles away at work on the morning that I ride through town with Maria Guadalupe. She's no longer that young girl of summer, but my mother, a woman in her late fifties, who smells of coconut-scented sunscreen and a stubborn fear, her nerves still rattled by the skin cancer recently removed from the bridge of her nose. This ride out to Los Ebanos was just an excuse to get out of the house.

Most of the houses here are made of clapboard or cinderblock. The smaller, mud brick and straw *jacales* seem slumped over with the pain of decalcified bones. At the local cemetery, the decorative arch proclaims *La Puerta*, and pink funeral bows are tied to the sagging chain-link fence.

My mother turns off at the sign for the ferry. The paved road becomes dirt. Up ahead, a line of dusty, Chevy pickup trucks and Crown Victorias with tinted windows are parked on the downward slope toward the river; they're waiting for the ferryboat, which is banked on the Mexican side. But we're not driving across. We haven't risked that since the late '70s.

We park under the shade of a mesquite, where a posted sign warns against carrying firearms into Mexico, and walk to the wooden shack that serves as a tollbooth. A man with an apron heavy with coins charges the 50 cents.

"It used to be a quarter," my mother gripes.

"Pues, ya no, señora," the man says. "Now it's 50 cents."

I hand over the dollar for both of us.

Across from the shack are the Border Patrol barracks. Two khakied agents sit outside waiting for the next load from Mexico. As my mother and I wait for cars to disembark and cars to board (the ferry takes no more than three cars per trip), we spot a pair of swim trunks discarded under the thick brush. The drawstring is knotted, the mesh lining bunched and crawling with ants.

The Mexico-bound cars start their engines. My mother hurries alongside, covering her nose and eyes against the up-churned dust, threatening to stumble and go head-over-tennis shoes into the dirt or the river.

"Uenas," she says to the ferrymen, as we set foot onto the metal ramp.

Down river, between the banks of the two countries, a flat-bottom boat cuts a silhouette against the glare off the water—*La Migra*. The agents are motionless as they watch us drift. The river current floats us to Mexico (which means crossers must swim against the current to get to the United States).

"How many cars pass back and forth each day?" my mother asks a ferryman.

He turns to the others for an estimate. When they don't answer, he shrugs, "Maybe around fifty."

"And why do you stop service at four o'clock?"

"Because that's a full day. From eight in the morning to four o'clock in the afternoon–that's eight hours."

"Right," my mother says, and then she looks at me with an arched brow to make sure I got that. Did she want me to write about this? About her?

She's been a vocal critic of my past work, but maybe she'll come around if I write about her?

She tells the ferryman that she used to ride this thing as a girl, on summer trips to the family ranch in Santa Gertrudis.

He nods and then joins the others who have distanced themselves from our leisure life. For them, this is just another workday. They are middle-aged Mexican-Mexicans, sunburned brown, who wear baseball caps and T-shirts. These are the kind of men who don't miss a day of work unless they wake up and find out that they have died during the night.

★

Unlike the visits my mother remembers from her childhood, there is no one waiting for us on the Mexican side. We walk up the embankment to the shade of a few trees, where a teen-aged vendor has set up a drink cart and a rack of peanuts and chili-spiced *chicharrón*. The sidewalk is studded with embedded bottle caps of Joya soft drinks and Carta Blanca beer. I take a Topo Chico mineral water. My mother turns to the vendor and the old men who sit nearby eating their lunch, and says, *"¡Hi'jesú!* I haven't been here in years."

My mother tells them about the ranch. She says that in the mornings, when she'd go fetch the *nixtamal* for the corn tortillas, the town boys would say, "Here comes the *gringuita*." She says it was because she was light-skinned. "I'd tell them, 'Not *gringa* and not anything but Mexican. *¡Soy mexicana!*'"

It's the first time I've heard my mother raise a little flag of Mexican pride. Usually she complains about all the Mexicans coming across to the United States.

One old man says he knows the ranch, which he calls *el ejido*. He offers a name—Martín—who turns out to be one of my mother's uncles.

Excited, she asks if it's still possible to get to Santa Gertrudis from here. A moment later, a grounds woman named Rosie, wearing chunky black sandals, capri khakis, and a PRI campaign T-shirt, pulls us to a taxi parked under the faded billboards for Don Pedro's and Parillada la Mela, restaurants that have since gone out of business.

"The economy," Rosie says, as if that explains everything.

She presents us to the driver of the first taxi, a yolk-yellow Grand Marquis, and tells him to give us a ride through Díaz Ordaz, the nearby town named after the buck-toothed leader who was president during the 1968 student massacre in Mexico City.

"Give them the sights," Rosie says.

"Un tour," agrees my mother.

With the way she forever warns me about the dangers of Mexico, I never expected her to agree to a taxi ride, but here she is, jumping into the back seat. Maybe the driver, because of his belly and bulk, reminds her of her fat *tío* Garcia.

I sit in front and roll the window down further, what we call "Mexican Aircon." From the rearview mirror hangs the driver's taxi license. I check to make sure it's our driver in the picture, and, yup, that's him, round faced and mustached, his name listed as Arturo Acosta Ramirez.

He starts the car and puts it in gear. We ease out onto a winding road, paved and desolate, edged by rich sorghum fields. Birds balance themselves on the stalks and pick at the heads of reddish grain. The bottle of Topo Chico sweats between my legs.

My mother, relaxed in the back seat, lets the air and sun hit her on the face. Since the cancer, she's been vigilant about staying out of the sun, slathering on the sunscreen and telling me how important it is to follow her lead since we're the light-skinned ones in the family. A moment later she props herself up between the seats and tells the driver about her childhood, crossing over on the ferry, a truck waiting to take them to Santa Gertrudis.

"El ejido," she says, picking up on what the old man had said. "You've heard of it?"

He shakes his head no and there is no more talk of the ranch.

We remain silent as we drive the two miles into town, where the central plaza looks like so many other small-town Mexican plazas: cement benches, a wrought-iron gazebo, anemic trees with white-painted trunks. There is no one around.

"It's the heat," says the driver. He points out the town church, San Miguel, facing the plaza, and where the driver says he made his first communion. It's also where his family sought refuge for eight days during Hurricane Beulah in 1967.

The driver pushes the taxi through the noon rush of the business district. The storefronts are crowded with "special offers" and "sales." The newer stores holler for attention over the sighs of the shadowy, shuttered businesses, where the signs have been removed and all that remain are the stencils of time and dust of what used to be. You can still read what was there years ago. Cine Acapulco. Cine 83. The driver says there isn't a single movie theater left.

We drive to one end of town, a slum where tennis shoes hang from the power lines and the skinny houses shouldering each other have their doors kicked open as if from a recent violence.

"The good thing about living in these houses is that if your neighbor decides to hang anything on his wall, you can take advantage of the nail when it pierces through to your side," the driver says. "You save yourself a nail."

On the cracked sidewalk an infant wanders in his underwear, alone, or so we think, until we spot the mother distracted by her other kids, or kids from the mothers who must be at work.

Teenage boys drift, cutting across from one dirt yard to another, wandering and seeming to wonder who we are in the slow-moving taxi. It begins to feel like a set-up. The taxi will stop and the hoodlums will descend on us and pull my mother and me out onto the streets and butcher us like those victims in the gruesome photo essays of *¡Alarma!* magazine.

Back on the main boulevard, still alive and relieved that this taxi driver wasn't steering us to an out of the way place to rob and kill us, I ask him about all the reported stories of murderous cab drivers in Mexico.

"That's only in Mexico City," he defends.

My mother believes it's going on everywhere. "I'm scared to go anywhere except right across the river to Las Flores," she admits. "Unless I have business, I don't go. Even Reynosa, which is just Reynosa—*¡ay!,* forget it."

"They knife you in broad daylight," the driver says, telling us of assailants who target taxi drivers. "Two will get on," he says, nodding in both my mother's and my directions, as if to place the two criminals where we are sitting. "I'm talking men. Two men will get into a taxi. One in back and one in front." He looks at me. "They direct him to a remote area, one of those neighborhoods in the outskirts, saying, 'Over there. Up ahead. Just a little farther.' And then they rob the guy."

He says he braves the work despite the police reports because he has a family to support and there's nowhere else to go. "I've lived here all my life," he explains. "Go anywhere else and you miss where you come from and it's just not worth the heartache."

Along the boulevard, schoolgirls wearing crisp white shirts and plaid skirts, walk home for lunch with long-stemmed roses in their hands. Other girls flock to the pushcarts selling candied yams and pumpkin. They stand under the shade of the striped orange canopies and fan away the bees as they point to the glass barrels of tamarind fruit juice and lemonade.

Back on the commercial strip, the driver slows and nods to a seafood restaurant named Vallarta. He asks if we are hungry for *camarones.* "It's the best shrimp in town," he says.

"I don't trust the food over here," my mother says. "It's not the same as what we got on the other side. You can get sick real ugly."

The driver doesn't insist, except to say that he brings loads of Winter Texans during the cold months. "They like it," he says, without really giving us the hard sell.

My mother finally thinks to ask the driver his name. *"Pa' la otra,"* she says, though I can't imagine a "next time."

Perhaps she cannot let go the idea of having someone, anyone—even a taxi driver—forever waiting for her on the other side.

★

Heading to the ferry, the river flowing alongside, the greenish water visible between the ebano trees, the driver tells us that lots of people drown. "They don't know how strong the current can be. You get a cramp. You stall in a whirlpool. That's it."

He also tells us about the ferry accident in the late '50s, when a taxi, carrying four women, nosed into the river and everyone drowned. Every story written about the ferry mentions this tragedy, some reporting four women died, other times three.

According to Acosta, one of the women panicked, startling their driver, causing him to hit the accelerator and send the car into the water.

★

Arriving at the ferry station, a soldier waves us through. Off to the side, a truck with Texas plates is being searched. Acosta parks under the faded billboards, next to the other taxi, a shiny Jetta. Rosie comes over to ask how it went and, I imagine, to collect her commission.

My mother and I head back to the river. A band has set up under the trees across from the snack and drink vendor. Rosie says the band plays whenever the mood strikes—which is apparently not right now.

A snare drum sits on its stand. A bass drum takes up part of the bench where the rest of the family of musicians sit in the swelter. One of the girls seems yoked by the saxophone hanging from her neck. A boy holds a battered and scaly trumpet across his lap. Still no music.

I pay for the return toll, but the ferrymen are taking their lunch break. My mother and I sit at one of the picnic tables and she asks Rosie, who rakes the ground, if the men are going to take the whole hour.

"N'hombre," Rosie says, looking over at them. "They never take more than ten minutes."

My mother tells her about the swim trunks we saw on the other side. She asks, "Does anyone ever try to get across?"

"Sure," Rosie says, going back to her rake and gathering cinders from a recent campfire. "They swim. A few try even with the Migra around. They're on a set schedule, which everyone knows, and so they're not always out there on patrol. Some even take the ferry across and as soon as they hit land they go off into the brush and cut through the mesquite and huizache. They say you come out at the Los Ebanos cemetery."

Behind us the band strikes up a whiny plaint of expired notes and drum beats.

"Do they know 'Paloma Negra'?" my mother asks Rosie.

Rosie is sure they can play it and asks if she should go make the request.

"No," my mother stops her. "I just wanted to know. I like the song is all."

Two middle-aged women approach and tell my mother that they are going to divine her luck and tell her the future. My mother shrieks and gets up. She lets out a string of "NOs," shaking her shoulders and stamping her feet as if to shake off a chill.

"*¡Qué susto!* Those things make me scared," my mother says, ignoring the women and giving them her back.

"There's nothing to be afraid of," the second woman says. "It's nothing bad."

The first woman eyes me. "How 'bout you, *joven?*"

My mother pulls me away. "*¡Ya! vámonos d'aquí.* I don't need nobody to tell me my future if I already have God."

My mother is a born-again Christian.

"That's right," says Rosie, who humors my mother with a hallelujiah.

As we head to the ferry, the band starts to play "Las Mañanitas."

★

My mother doesn't need to know the future when she has the past to keep her happy. She recalls the early morning errands for the *nixtamal*. She also remembers the ranch house—the kitchen with the dirt floors and the walls made of dried mud, the wool blankets for the night chill. On weekends, the boys from the neighboring ranches came to the windows to sing "Las Mañanitas" to the girls.

Other weekend nights they held dances at the local school. Strings of colored paper were hung, which the girls and boys picked, and the boys came around later to compare colors.

"They'd show you the little paper," my mother says. "If they matched, you had to dance the first song together. But just the first song. After that it was up to you whether you wanted to keep dancing with the same guy or choose someone else."

There were other games, too, like greasing a thick pole with animal fat and planting a flag at the top. "I never found out who got the flag," she says, and she forgets what it was you won.

Of the family at Santa Gertrudis, she recalls the bachelor uncle, Augustín, who liked to play the accordion and guitar: "They say that a woman left him and he never wanted another."

Her Aunt Virginia didn't marry until she was so old that most of her teeth had already fallen out and she kept wads of cotton in her mouth to fill out her collapsed cheeks. Not that it kept her from being an unapologetic gossip. Whenever she spoke of anyone she referred to them as "that lazy so-and-so."

My mother says her cousin Olga married a jealous man who shut her in the house and brushed the dirt around the front door with a mesquite branch so that later he could check for tracks. He didn't want anyone coming in and out of the house while he was gone.

My mother stopped going to Mexico at the age of 13, when she became old enough to work, and her summers were filled with cotton and tomato fields. The only time she went back to the ranch was for the funerals.

"Over there the caskets are fitted with glass," she tells me. "You see them dead, but you don't touch them."

No kissing their cold cheek or their liver-spotted hands? That was a ritual my mother forced us to do. Until now I always thought it was a Mexican thing. But it must be my mother's way of sending off our loved ones with the hope that they will be waiting for us on the other side of whatever lies beyond this life.

★

Back on the job, the ferrymen wave two U.S.-bound trucks forward a few more inches to make room for a third pickup they call *la güerita*, refer-ring either to its pale color or to the light-skinned, bleached-blond Mexican woman at the wheel. All three trucks have their windows rolled down and the drivers rest their elbows on the chrome sills.

My mother and I stand against the ferry railing and watch the dragonflies disturb the river surface with the dip of their tails. *La Migra* is nowhere in sight. For a moment, it's as if there are no borders, as if this *norteño* homeland was still undivided.

Working in tandem, the four ferrymen lean forward and pull on the rope with their gloved hands. A pulley squeaks against a greased guide rope. The men grunt. The water slaps the lip of the ferry, pushing aside leaves and twigs and trailing a delicate wake of foam. The ride has been clocked at three to five minutes. For my mother it must feel like a lifetime passing.

It isn't until we are midway across the river that we notice our cab driver standing alone on the opposite side of the ferry. My mother waves to get his attention. She hollers that she just remembered that a cousin of hers died in the nearby river of Comales. "Her car fell into the water and she drowned," she says.

Acosta nods without comment. What could he say? When the ferry docks, he walks ahead, as if to get away.

He is fatter than I first thought, his white shirt too tight, the epaulets ready to pop.

At the checkpoint, a vaguely antagonistic sign welcomes us to the United States of America. The agent checks Acosta's "papers"—a single laminated card that he pulls out halfway from his wallet and then puts back into his worn back pocket, where there's a shotgun-sized hole.

The agent is Mexican-American, like us. He asks my mother and me if we're American citizens. I say yes. My mother says, "Yessir, I'm an American!"— just as proudly as she had said, *"Soy mexicana."*

RECUERDO: MY SISTER REMEMBERED

In the picture, my sister, Michelle, sits in her wrought-iron throne, and her long white gown drops to the wood floor of the rental hall. It is her fifteenth birthday. She's a *señorita* now. In my mind though, she will forever remain a teenage princess, dead before she was able to fulfill her promise as a woman in the world. She holds a bouquet of pink ribbon and carnations. My mother wears a matching corsage pinned to her rust-colored dress. My kid brother, Marco, stands taller than most of us, wearing slacks, a button-down shirt, and cowboy boots in dusty shades of brown. My baggy shirt and pants shimmer with the iridescence of middle-child neglect. Behind me, forced into a pale gray suit, my father stands with his shirt open at the collar. His mustache is dark. His hair brushed back. He faces the camera with his eyes closed, as if he wants to forget this night, or the more terrible night that will come later and stamp a permanent shadow over the family. For now we are caught in the glare of a photographer's flashbulb.

★

Many years later, while I am home on a visit, I sit in the gloom of the dining room of my parents' new house. The shades are drawn against the hot summer afternoon. This is the Valley, where most of my family still lives, and where the sun shines more than three hundred days out of the year. I moved away years ago and only come back for the memories.

I flip through the photo album the hired photographer had prepared for my sister's quinceañera. My father, now in his sixties, his hair and mustache gone gray, looks at himself in photo after photo and doesn't know what became of that suit. He scratches at the collar of his V-neck undershirt, at the tattoos that have turned green, remembering a much earlier night as a teenager, when he escorted a quinceañera.

"One of my ex-girlfriends," he says. He laughs and then mutters that he shouldn't say more because "your mom gets mad."

My mother, who used to pay me a nickel when I was a kid for each white hair I plucked from her head, would be completely gray now, too, if it weren't for the dye she works into her curls every couple of months. Overhearing us, she comes in from another part of the house and asks, "Get mad? *Porque me voy poner* mad?"

When I tell her, she shakes her head and sighs, *"Déjalo que diga."*

Not like my father remembers all that much anyway. He can't even recall his girlfriend's first name, just the last. "Martinez," he says. "We were going steady."

He was either sixteen or seventeen or eighteen. He's not even sure of that. But she was younger and then, the way he tells it, "The dreaded moment came." Martinez turned fifteen and needed a *chambelán* to escort her at her *quince*.

My father remembers that instead of a tuxedo he wore a "regular blue suit."

"I don't know from where," my mother cracks. She's always considered him a horrible dresser, the kind of man who wears white athletic socks with dress shoes.

"I dunno if I borrowed it or what, *pero* I had a suit," he defends. "It was kind of a bluish suit."

My father says he really didn't want to go through with it. "I was from the *rancho*," he explains, meaning that he didn't live in town like his girlfriend. Growing up in the outlying community of Madero, he lived among recent arrivals from across the river who settled and raised families and worked at the German-owned brick factory nearby, which everyone called the Little Prison. On weekends, in your neighbor's backyard, cow heads slow-cooked in ember-filled holes in the ground. My father, who was born and raised along the muddy banks of the Rio Grande, says he doesn't remember any of the local girls holding a quinceañera. His sister Lucy never had one.

"It was a city thing," he says. The other thing, he adds, "I was not a good dancer. That was the worst part. I had to be the first one dancing."

He lets out a low whistle as he tries to remember where the reception was held. It may have been at Mitla Patio, the south-side hall where most of the weekend dances were held at the time, but he's not certain. "No, I think it was at the convention center." Only there is no "convention center" in town. He must mean the community center at Lion's Park. "Yeah," he says, more sure of himself now. "I think it was the community center."

Then, all at once, he remembers his girlfriend's name was Norma Linda Martinez. But he's still not sure about where the reception had been held. Maybe it was at the Mitla after all. The lights strung overhead. The bandstand which he used to crawl under when he was a kid to watch the folks dance and, the empty lot in the back where he and his friends played *canicas*—games of marbles with names like *el hoga'o* and *la chusa.*

My father knows more about the strategies and rules for shooting marbles than stories about Norma Linda Martinez because when I press him for more memories he says he doesn't have any.

"Nothing," he insists. *"Na'a."*

It's not so easy forgetting the night of my sister's quinceañera. A framed picture stands on the living room coffee table. My father sees it every day—my sister posed between him and my mother—and he says he feels numb. "I don't think. I don't wish. I don't—nothing," he says. "I just look at it."

★

My mother reminds me that I was a *chambelán* once. I'm not sure what year that was, but she says, *"Allá 'sta el retrato,"* as if the picture will do the hard work of remembering.

I recall the afternoon I raced from a friend's house on my ten-speed so that I could get home and get dressed in time to make the reception. Finally, a date with Iris, my junior high school crush, though we both were in high school by then.

I shot through an intersection, under a traffic light turning red, and when I next looked up to see what was ahead, I saw the shiny chrome grille of an oncoming diesel truck. I swerved left.

The emergency room doctor said I was fine. My bike and I had slammed into a cement irrigation pipe, but I hadn't broken anything, or suffered much of a concussion. I'd passed out on impact but was immediately woken up by a high-pitched scream from a witness who'd seen the whole thing while pulling up to the drive-thru window of the Whataburger across the street.

After the check up at the hospital, I went home and put on my rented tux, snapped on the aquamarine bow tie and cummerbund, passed a cloth over my spit-shined shoes, and headed to the dance.

There are pictures of me wearing a white boutonniere in my buttonhole. Iris was cinched into a tight cocktail dress layered with lace, white gloves, pumps and a veiled pillbox hat.

Otherwise, I remember nothing.

★

My mother spent most of her girlhood stooped over a sun-beaten cotton row and, at the end of a blistering work day that began at dawn and ended at dusk, went home to a tar-papered house where the drinking water was drawn in buckets from the surrounding irrigation canals. She was a champion picker who harvested a thousand pounds of cotton in a single day. Or so she says. Her picture appeared in the local paper. Just never to announce the occasion of her quinceañera.

"I don't even remember when I turned fifteen," she says. "I never took my years seriously, like saying, 'Hey, tomorrow's my birthday.' *No le ponía cuida'o.*"

But she remembers the first time a guy came to her house to call on her. "I still played with dolls *en ese tiempo y yo lloré cuando me nombró.*" She says a sister-in-law told her, "*Oye*, you're already a *señorita.* It's time for men to come calling." But my mother cried no. "*Todavía no*—I still considered myself a little girl."

My mother would've been fifteen in 1959, but she doesn't recall anything in particular about that year. "*Como te digo, no me recuerdo nada porque* most of the time I was always working. I had to drop outta school to work in the fields. To help out. Mom was sick of nerves. Sick of her heart. So *que servia que supiera* that it was my birthday? There wasn't gonna be any gifts. I wasn't gonna have a party. I just lived my life working in the fields and taking care of Mom and that was it. I was happy."

She worked hard and her only pleasures consisted of swimming in the canals, running through sprinklers, and standing in the rain. My mother always thought she'd make a great mermaid.

Still, she claims she was a *dama* for other quinceañeras, and she explains that she'd buy fabric at the downtown dry goods and then take it to the appointed seamstress, who made the dresses for the entire court of *damas*. "At the time it was cheap. It's not as bad as it is now. *Ahora te sale bien caro. Bien* 'spensive. A lot of people don't go with the *damas* anymore because a lot of them don't have the money, or the hassle *con la costurera, que los vestidos no quedaron bien. Y luego despues los chambelanes no todos quieren pagar.*"

Unlike my father, who wore that bluish suit for his *chambelán* duties, my mother says all of her escorts wore tuxedos. She recalls lining up with her date and standing under a flower-decorated arch as the *damas* and *chambelanes* were announced. The way she tells it, the presentation started with a one-year-old *dama* and her escort (I don't know whether to believe my mother, but she goes on) then the two-year-olds, and so on.

"*Las* girls *p'acá, y los* boys *p'allá—hasta la que tenía* fourteen. *Y luego al último, la quinceañera sola con su chambelán. Bailaban el primer vals. Bailaba con el papá. Y luego al rato bailábamos todos.*"

★

My sister's quinceañera was my mother's idea. Maybe, since my sister was born on my mother's birthday, December 28, my mother also wanted to celebrate her fifteenth, twenty-four years late. So in less than a month, and with a budget that amounted to weeks of my mother's wages as a grocery store cashier, my mother and sister put the event together, setting the date for the last day of the year, the eve of 1984.

A local printer designed the invitations in Spanish, which none of us kids could read well. And the picture of my sister they used for the front of the invite turned out looking like an amateur photocopy job of gray tones and streaks.

Aunt Ofelia lent my sister the three-hundred-dollar dress our cousin Nani had worn a year earlier. "Just take it to the cleaners," Ofelia said.

On the big night, my mother helped my sister into the white dress—silk bodice, scalloped neckline, and puffy shoulders that tapered to the wrists. My mother had heard that "*las perlas eran malas*"—pearls were bad luck—that whoever wore them would end up crying later, but she didn't want to believe the superstition as she clasped a string of pearls around my sister's neck and then adjusted her matching earrings.

A family friend picked up my sister at our old house in a burgundy Lincoln Continental decorated with pink streamers and a quinceañera doll lashed to the hood ornament. My sister, sitting alone in the backseat, rode out of the *colonia*. Past the wood homes squatting on crumbling bricks. Homes without proper water or sewer lines so that a stink arose whenever the backyard septic tanks overflowed. Homes that were boarded up in the summer when families went north, following the harvest seasons for strawberries and corn. Homes where the neighborhood girls called one another "stuck ups" for thinking they were better than this. Homes where the dogs prowled about glistening from baths of burned motor oil that was supposed to cure them of the mange.

The Lincoln Continental left all this behind as it made its way around the potholes and headed towards town and the early evening Mass at St. Paul's. From outside, the concrete church, with its high arched ceiling, has always looked like a holy airport hangar. Inside, a huge copper and brass crown floated over the altar. My kid brother fantasized, as he did most Sundays during Mass, "What if the crown fell on the priest?"

My mother and father escorted my sister down the aisle to the altar railing, where she knelt on a fringed pillow embroidered with the sentiment MIS XV AÑOS.

The first three pews, reserved for family, had been decorated with flowers, but since this was a regular Saturday night Mass, most of the church was flocked with "Snow Birds"—white-haired retirees from the Midwest who migrated south to play shuffle board through the warm winter. "*Se miraban asustados,*" my mother notes. "Like they'd never seen a quinceañera before."

Most likely they hadn't.

The reception was held at the church hall next door, which we decorated with pink streamers, and filled with the melodies of "Happy Birthday" and "Las Mañanitas." We ate on the butcher-paper-covered folding tables.

Other families pitched in with side dishes of Spanish rice and beans *a la charra* that smelled of bacon fat and cilantro and garlic (to ease the gas). Our family provided the main course of barbecue brisket. My mother doesn't know where she bought it. "*La mera verdad no me 'cuerdo—pero* I think I bought it in McAllen or Mission." She thinks a moment. "Ramiro? Ramiro's Meat Market?" She's not sure. "*Allá pa' rumbo* Palmview. The man already died from diabetes. They chopped off one leg. Then they chopped off the other. Then his wife died of stomach cancer."

The cake was baked in Edinburg. My mother doesn't know where, though she recalls that it was three tiers tall, the layers filled with pineapple. The *pan de polvo* came from the bakery at the H.E.B. supermarket where my mother worked.

The Barbie doll *muñeca* that sat near the cake came from the widow who lived in the *colonia* with her unmarried daughters. There was also a guest book *RECUERDOS DE MIS XV AÑOS*, but nobody signed it because we forgot to put it out.

My sister posed for photos: Michelle with her lace parasol. Michelle with her school friend Maritza, who was the only friend she invited because, my mother explained then, "We can't afford to entertain everyone." Michelle with family and family friends—Chapa, Garza, Guerra, Ortiz, Perez, Riojas and Tanguma. The women wore borrowed dresses and blouses and sucked in their stomachs so that they wouldn't look too fat. The men wore stretchy dress pants and boots with matching cowboy hats, smiling as if they wanted to let loose but wouldn't.

My sister had long black hair, which at times she blow-dried straight or burned into tight curls with a hot iron as she did that night. When my mother had the money, and even when she didn't, she took my sister to the M&H Beauty Salon, with its narcotic smell of hair dyes and styling products. My brother and I sat on the floor by the old-lady beehive hair-dryers and watched my sister get her spiral perms.

When girls sprayed their bangs into a high bird's crest, my sister used an entire can of Aqua Net and then walked to the school bus stop facing the wind's direction. She walked without seeing where she was going, her neck turning like a weather vane, so that her hair wouldn't get blown out of place. She was always a stumble away from disaster.

Her legs bowed like Grandma 'Torina's. And she was obsessed with a "bump" on the bridge of her nose, which she swore she'd fix as soon as she got famous. A wart grew on the inside of one nostril, perhaps from obsessing so much, and my brother and I watched the family doctor cauterize the monster. She also suffered from ingrown hairs under her arm, which she suspected were tumors and cried as my mother put warm compresses on the pimples and, with a sterilized needle, lanced and drained them and told her no, she was not dying.

For her big night, my sister didn't have a live band. No mariachi. No DJ. Instead, we spun our own records: Michael Jackson's *Off the Wall*, the *Flashdance* soundtrack, and Laura Branigan with her ballad of grief "How Am I Supposed to

Live Without You." They were the hot sounds that year.

My mother says that my sister would've liked a formal dance—unless it was her own dancing feet trying to convince her—but my father didn't want anything. *"Tu papá así es—bien avergüenzoso,"* my mother gripes more than two decades later. *"El no quería na'a.* Period. Like always. He never wants nothing."

★

Not like they did anything for my birthday earlier that same year, when I finally became a teenager at thirteen. You'd think that my being born on their wedding anniversary would help them remember.

I remained at the kitchen table long after dinner was done, sat there waiting for someone in my family to say "Happy Birthday." As everyone went off to bed, my mother, ready to turn out the kitchen light, came up and told me, *"Ya, duérmete."* I didn't move. She asked, *"¿Pos qué te pasa, huerco?"*

I started to cry in the dark, letting out these very un-grown-up gasps, telling her that it was my birthday and nobody remembered.

Everyone got out of bed and climbed into the El Camino and we drove down the road to the Sunshine convenience store. They were about to close, but the counter guy let us in and as everyone waited in the car, I wandered the fluorescent-lit aisles, looking at the racks of fried pocket pies, and their stock of pre-packaged goods from the Butter Crust Bakery.

I picked out a German chocolate cake wrapped in cellophane and blue-plaid cardboard. It wasn't even the whole cake. Only half. They sold it in half and quarter portions. For a long time afterward I loved German chocolate cake.

★

My parents went on forgetting my birthday. A kid as ignored as me would've run away from home a long time ago, but it was my sister who always threatened to leave as soon as she graduated high school.

We lived in Mission, a town of twenty-five thousand, famous for being home of the Ruby Red grapefruit and the birthplace of Dallas Cowboys football coach Tom Landry. My sister wanted a bigger and more glamorous life away from all that. My brother and I didn't know what she had to complain about since she was the favorite. She got the latest Gloria Vanderbilts and Sergio Valentes. So what if they were from K-Mart. My sister even had her own room—well, we did too, but it just wasn't the same—with her canopy bed, pre-op Michael Jackson posters, and walls the color of pink flamingos on fire.

In high school, Michelle danced with the High Flyers, the majorettes who dressed as cowgirls with tasseled white boots, ruffled skirts, vests, and gloves. At the Friday night football games, they tipped their cowboy hats at the start of every half-time show. My sister languished among the ranks for two years before she made the more visible cheerleading squad. She hollered and shook her maroon pom-poms at the games. If our team, the Eagles, wasn't doing well, the cheerleaders snapped out their double-jointed arms and stiffened their hands into talons and hissed the battle cry, "Eagle Claw." The other popular cheer was called "Go Fight Win," which they did to the accompaniment of the marching band.

GO. GO-GO.
GO, MIGHTY EAGLES.
FIGHT. FIGHT-FIGHT.
FIGHT, MIGHTY EAGLES.
WIN. WIN-WIN.
WIN, MIGHTY EAGLES.
GO, GO, GO, FIGHT, FIGHT, FIGHT, WIN!

My sister was a spirited high school student who was junior class president, head of the prom committee, and was on staff at the school paper and yearbook. After school, she worked as a cashier at the Mission H.E.B. supermarket. On weekends, she volunteered at the Retama Nursing Home in McAllen. Like most teenagers, she was busy with life. And she was my sister. Diana Michelle Guerra.

★

The last time I saw her alive, she was sitting on my twin bed, in the yellowish light of my room, watching me pack a suitcase. It was the summer of '87. The radio wept with ballads of displacement like "Somewhere Out There," by Ronstadt and Ingram, or it rocked with the power chords of

"Alone" by the sister duo Heart. I was seventeen and going away to Florida to stay with cousins. I planned to get a summer job at Disney World.

My sister, eighteen, had just graduated from high school. Her plan was to go to North Texas State in Denton, to study I don't know what, since she was always changing her mind. She wanted to be a veterinarian, a high-fashion model in Paris or Milan, or an actress on *General Hospital* or *Guiding Light*. She had the dizzy and un-disciplined aspirations that everyone has in their youth. Mostly, she wanted to get away, and she howled her entire short life that she couldn't wait to escape.

Our parents wanted her to stay put and attend Pan American University (which all of us called "Taco Tech"), because it was less than ten miles from our house, and because she was a girl. She would be safer here.

My sister had not been anywhere on her own other than the cheerleading camps in San Antonio and Dallas, which had been chaperoned by squad sponsors. There was a Spring Break trip her senior year to Puerto Vallarta, but that had been with my mother, and the report back was that they had fought. One of my sister's favorite arguments, as she got older and demanded she be allowed to go where she wanted, was to say, "If I'm gonna die, I'm gonna die." Her teenage fatalism never convinced our parents. More than anything, they were shocked by her desperate, almost suicidal challenge to be let out into the world.

★

In July, I bought a postcard and wrote my sister, encouraging her to come to Florida to audition for one of the Disney shows. But I never got the chance to mail it. The night of the Fourth, returning from my job at the Pecos Bill Cafe in Frontierland, I felt homesick and alone. My cousins were at a barbecue. I stayed in, feeling sorry for myself, which my sister would not have approved.

Later, as I tried to sleep, the neighbors fired guns and set off fireworks in celebration of our independence. A dog howled throughout the night.

Mexicans believe the superstition that dogs howl when someone you know has died. I felt the passing of my own childhood into adulthood. Only it wasn't the orchestrated flowering that a woman experiences at fifteen, coming into her own with the blessings of the church, her family and friends. I, like most men, did it alone and without ceremony.

I lay in bed and recalled past July Fourths when my brother and sister and I made our parents buy us bottle rockets and smoke bombs. We lit sparklers at the kitchen stove and ran through the hall and out the door as my mother screamed about the house catching fire. When my parents fell asleep, we snuck into the fridge and took a can of my father's Lone Star and passed it around.

Early the following morning my cousins knocked on my bedroom door and said my mother was on the phone. Then I knew. The dog from last night.

When I got to the phone, all I heard was my mother's choked crying. "They took her," she said.

★

I flew home the next day. When I arrived, the sheriff's department had questioned everyone from family to neighbors to current and past boyfriends to suspicious uncles who they felt were too interested in what had been found so far. Which was nothing. Michelle was still missing.

I drove my father's truck into town and put up flyers with pictures of my sister and the question: HAVE YOU SEEN HER?

Later, I rode to a house where a group of my sister's friends had gathered to pray, and I stood alone with my brother, as my sister's boyfriend and her best friend cried together on the living room couch. When the crowd dispersed, everyone going home to dinner and the rest of their lives, a call came through from an uncle telling my brother and me to get home.

"Did you find her?" I said on the phone. "Is she all right?"

He refused to say anything specific, just that we should get home, now.

Outside, as we looked for a ride, a brown car came screeching down the street and almost came up onto the yard. The car rocked back and forth as it came to a stop. The girl, another of my sister's friends—she had so many—flung the door open and shouted that they had found my sister.

"They found Michelle," she cried, and before taking another breath she said that my sister was dead.

My knees buckled. I fell onto the grass. White clouds drifted in the burning sky and I felt the heat taking me, taking me, taking me into its arms in a way that all of my sister's friends had failed to do.

★

They found my sister in a pasture behind our house. The summer heat had badly decomposed her body. The local news stations broadcast grainy video clips of her skinny cheerleader's arm jutting out of the tall dry grass.

For someone who had such far-flung dreams—and this is the part that makes my heart ache most—her life came to this nightmare end not far from home, where she was supposed to be the safest. They never found her killer. The case went cold.

★

After high school, I moved away without really moving on. My sister's friends attended college near and far; they married and tacked on their husband's last names; they became registered nurses and teachers and mothers. In my own family, the next generation of cousins continues to celebrate their passage into womanhood. They now spend up to a year and thousands of dollars to plan and pay for the event. They order their triple-tier cakes and sugary *pan de polvo* cookies from the Celebrity bakery in McAllen. They buy their dresses and tiaras from the Princess shop in Palmview. They rent Nellie's Ballroom, the Villa Real Convention Center or the Outta Town Dance Hall. They pay up to two hundred dollars to print a two-hundred word announcement in the local newspaper.

★

Dear Michelle, On my last trip back home, Mom takes me on a drive through Valley Memorial Gardens. She points out the new section where she has moved herself and Dad, leaving the two plots on either side of you for Marco and me to escort you into eternal rest.

Mom, once busy making a perfect home, now prepares us for the afterlife. She insists, "*La muerte de segura la tiene uno. Por mas que uno no quiere hablar de la muerte*, you have to know that everybody someday will have to leave. Nobody is gonna stay. *Un día como quiera te tienes que ir al otro mundo.*"

The sprinklers shoot weepy arcs of water over the grounds. We don't get out of the truck to see you. We don't have to. From the countless trips we've made to your grave, we've memorized the inscription on the marker: "She shared her smiles and hid her tears."

Mom kisses her fingers and waves them toward you and whispers, "Love you, *m'hija.*"

She points out the nearby tree that was planted around the time of your burial. It now casts a shadow over your grave in the afternoon.

"She don't have to be in the sun that much," Mom murmurs, forgetting that you always wanted to be in the sun, to shine under a Hollywood spotlight.

Pointing out the distance between the graves where you and Marco and I will eventually lay, and where she and Dad will be buried, Mom says she didn't want us ending up too far away from one another. She wants to keep us together forever. She wonders aloud, "You think I did right by changing?"

She's still not sure. But one thing is certain. This is the end of the line for us Guerras. Marco and I are both unmarried and childless. There's no one to carry on our name. Soon, instead of a family remembered, we will be a family forgotten. "Remember the Guerras," they'll say, and no one will.

Later, Mom drives to the old church, where you took your First Communion, celebrated your quinceañera, and where we held your funeral services. As we get off the truck, Mom grumbles that she should have brought her hat. She puts a folded newspaper over her head instead. "I gotta protect myself," she says, concerned ever since the skin cancer diagnosis a few years ago. "I'm not gonna let the sun get to me."

We try the heavy doors to both the church and the new parish hall—the old one was demolished—but they're locked. We're not sure where to go next. What doors of memory are left?

The palms sway in the summer breeze and the anacuahita trees drop their white trumpet flowers that burn on the hot sidewalk. A flock of wild parrots bursts into the sky, their green feathers glimmering in the sun as they swoop and squawk. I never knew parrots roosted in the Valley, but Mom says, "They come from Mexico— they cross."

I want to think there are fifteen altogether, but I lose count after twelve. By Mom's estimate they are merely a bunch. "Look," she whispers to herself, "there they go."

The birds flutter past in an emerald blur, between the tall palms and over the nearby park, the flock unraveling and disappearing into the sky.

ACKNOWLEDGMENTS

I'd like to thank the editors who first published these pieces: Barbara Belejack, Dagoberto Gilb, Daisy Hernandez, Adriana Lopez, Jake Silverstein.

Many thanks to my Thursday night group who helped shape these stories and countless others. Victoria Grantham for opening up her home each week. Aly Gerber for that final push and polish. For always being there with wine and wisdom: Sarah Showfety, Joe Antol, Royal Young, Jennifer Tang, Shani Friedman. Thanks, guys.

Thank you, Sue Shapiro, for being such a generous teacher and connecting us to one another.

Thank you to my family of literary sisters: Maria Límon, Anel Flores and Michelle Otero.

I'm grateful for the fellowship at the Macondo Writers' Workshop and the love and guidance from my literary madrina Sandra Cisneros.

Thanks to Macarena Hernandez and Edgar Sandoval. You two keep me going and keep me rooted.

Eileen Cho, Kam Lau and Joselyn Martinez, you three have been there since the beginning and I want to thank you for sticking by me all these years. You don't know how important each of you has been to me.

Thank you, Radis Jensethawat, for refuge, silliness and companionship.

I'd like to thank my family. Dad and Marco, thanks for sharing your life and stories with me. Michelle, who only wanted the best for herself and her kid brothers, I'll never forget what you taught me. Mom, who has shared so much of herself with me, who has since learned the phrase "this is off the record," these stories are for you.

About the Author

ERASMO GUERRA was born and raised on the Texas-Mexico border. His nonfiction stories have appeared in *The New York Times, Texas Monthly, The Texas Observer* and aired on NPR. His work has been honored with a Lambda Literary Award and he has received writing grants from the Vermont Studio Center, The Fine Arts Work Center and the Virginia Center for the Creative Arts. He is a member of the Macondo Writers' Workshop and lives in New York City.

Made in the USA
Middletown, DE
01 July 2022